About the Authors

I am Meccia Griggs McCants, a proud educator and writer. I am hard working, enjoy chilling, and finding time to connect pen to paper.
I have been married for nineteen years and look forward to many more. Please enjoy our work.

I am Jizammie J. Griggs, an author. I long to leave my mark in this world in which I love! May God guide your steps as he has mine.

This is a work of fiction. Names, characters, businesses, places, events and incidents are either the products of the author's imagination or used in a fictitious manner. Any resemblance to actual persons, living or dead, or actual events is purely coincidental.

BLOOD POETRY

Jizammie J. Griggs
and
Meccia Griggs McCants

BLOOD POETRY

Vanguard Press

VANGUARD PAPERBACK

© Copyright 2022
Jizammie J. Griggs and Meccia Griggs McCants

The right of Jizammie J. Griggs and Meccia Griggs McCants to be identified as authors of this work has been asserted by them in accordance with the Copyright, Designs and Patents Act 1988.

All Rights Reserved

No reproduction, copy or transmission of this publication may be made without written permission.
No paragraph of this publication may be reproduced, copied or transmitted save with the written permission of the publisher, or in accordance with the provisions of the Copyright Act 1956 (as amended).

Any person who commits any unauthorised act in relation to this publication may be liable to criminal prosecution and civil claims for damages.

A CIP catalogue record for this title is available from the British Library.

ISBN 978 1 80016 513 7

*Vanguard Press is an imprint of
Pegasus Elliot Mackenzie Publishers Ltd.*
www.pegasuspublishers.com

First Published in 2022

**Vanguard Press
Sheraton House Castle Park
Cambridge England**

Printed & Bound in Great Britain

Dedication

This book, *Blood Poetry*, is dedicated to our mom,
Alice M. Griggs
"We thank you for instilling in our minds and hearts
Goodness"

Also, I would like to dedicate this book, *Blood Poetry*,
to my sister,
Meccia Griggs McCants
And I would like to say
"Because of you, I will always have a friend, and so
will you!"

It is so beneficial to make your siblings your best
friends
We have a saying my siblings and I
"We're all we got"

A Mother's Love
By: Jizammie J. Griggs

A mother's love, is love in its purest form, why! Just the sound of her voice could calm you through the most catastrophic of storms,
and that voice will stay with you as you age and grow,
and even when she's gone it will never let you go,
because a mother is love and love is God,
so pay homage because that's how you got your start,
she's the birther of life, and your protector,
so while she is still here with you now,
don't neglect her!
Show her love, always respect her and always have her back,
because the moral to this poem, is that's the only mother you get.

> Happy Mother's Day
> Ma, I love you!

Pen and Paper
By: Meccia Griggs McCants

Pen and paper is where I live.
Words they flow like blood I've spilled.
Bringing works to life, showing who I am for real.
Each word a tear, a smile, a friend, a love past-present,
A sin outlived, a joy that's gained; my fortune and fame, the start, the finish; making me winner of the game.
Every word is different; blood makes them the same, the life that flows from me — the works that live again.

Pen and Paper
By: Jizammie J. Griggs

These words I've mastered, unlike friends,

This, relationship I foster, has no end,

I get to share, my deepest thoughts,

These words, they never highlight my faults,

I get to be, who I really am,

These words I write, don't give a damn!

I think there's ink, inside my blood,

That makes me so, at one with words,

No ridicule, no judgment, just pen and paper,

Solitude is great and these words are my staple.

Captured
By: Meccia G. McCants

Dearly beloved, anchor from fear.

Totally captured, I die freely here.

No strength of my own, your heart is my home.

I give all myself: blood, flesh, will and bones.

Unlike in times past, you leave or you stay.

I'm completely captured, til angels fly me away.

Freedomless
By: Jizammie J. Griggs

Should I falter, should I be captured,

Should I give in and die; I could only pray,

That a woman like you,

Would be the one to catch my eye,

For I know I would be in good hands,

You would claim me as your own,

Mold me into a good man,

And make me a happy home,

Bear my fruitful seeds and never leave my side,

And love me till my tired body,

Has weltered up and died.

But this wouldn't be my first death,

For my soul died way before,

I had the spirit of a free man who was captured a long time ago.

Midnight's Cry
By: Meccia Griggs McCants
MGM (Melagriggs2002)

Time will not share you with me.
Demons scream we are not meant to be.
Angels' tears fall like missing years;
and you are far away tonight.
Heaven's stars hide their faces,
as the wind's love turns away its graces.
I am trapped in pain's cry
and still all you feed me are lies.
Time will not share you with me,
The demons scream we are not meant to be;
but one touch can bring me back to peace.

Desti ination (dest•ti•na•tion)
By: Jizammie J. Griggs

Separation Creates Destiinations,
You're my Destiination,
And I'm your Destiination,
And one day we will close the empty,
Miles of space between us,
And like magic the asphalt, fields, mountains, and sky,
Will all disappear and we will stand,
Aura to aura,
Finally reunited,
Absent of any and all obstacles,
And on the brink of any and all possibilities!
I am your Destiination! And you are mine!

Beguilement
By: Meccia La'Tara Griggs

Heedless I placed me in your hands,
Looking to be loved purely.
Saged not to your past, that states,
"I have no grace in your world."
I became the secret kept never to be revealed,
Yet betrayed by deceit, that as the sea by the moon,
turned on itself.
How naive my narcissistic view
that you could make common your love.
for my singleness plus you.

Why, the biggest obstacle in life,
is one's self.
Jizammie J. Griggs

SELF
By: Jizammie J. Griggs

As a young man, I thought I knew everything,

I mean no one could tell me anything,

From the advice that I was given,

To the wisdom I ignored,

I was blinded by self,

My empty glass had no room,

My entire being, ego had consumed,

But if you live you learn,

Or so I've been told,

But my self-righteous attitude,

Had firmly taken hold,

I would leap first,

And then complain about the landing,

Now I can only thank God,

That today I am still standing.

Fright Night
A short story by Meccia Griggs McCants

We had some fun, wild and adventurous times as youth. One of the most memorable was 'Fright Night'. Basically, one of us would be blindfolded in a dark room or house and the other three would hide. Yeah, I know, sounds like hide-and-seek, but you had to be there to understand just how frightening things could get. One fall evening, we were left home, while the adults went out on the town. We were given two rules, the first rule was, don't open the door, and the second rule was, don't tear down the house. Well, we could definitely do both of these things but the night was yet to reveal itself completely.

    We waited the proper forty-five minutes to be sure, there was no backtracking by the parents and then the fun started.

    Terrell, our rebellious brother, spoke what we all were thinking. "Let's play Fright Night, not it!" he yelled. But he was too late; we had fled the room before he could complete his thought. "No fair!" he roared.

    He found one of Momma's scarves and tied it around his eyes. Then we heard footsteps; he was on the hunt. Just as he was about to reach out and touch Jay, the eldest of my brothers, there was a rattle at the door. The house felt deathly silent, I even noticed I was holding my breath. We all started to move very slowly and quietly to the back closest because it was huge and all of us could fit inside of it.

"Did you hear that?" Jay asked.

"Yeah," said Derrell, who is the baby of the bunch. "We going to get a whipping," he whined.

"No we are not," I said. "If that was Momma she'd be in here by now."

"Shhh," said Jay. "I hear it again."

"What we going to do Jay?" Terrell asked, with a bat in his hand. Funny, but in the moments we had been together, that was the first time we saw he had a
bat. We fell out laughing.

"Terrell said he ain't playing," Jay remarked rubbing a tear from his eye.

Then we heard the sound again. This time it was at the back door.

"What are we going do man?" Terrell asked while picking up his bat again.

"Let's peek out the window," I suggested while moving closer to the back of the group. We all tipped to the window just in time to see a shadow go by. I almost screamed but being the only girl in the group, I didn't want my brothers to think I was a punk. So I bit my hand and tried to hold back the tears; that hurt worse than I meant it to.

Jay called us all together and whispered, "I don't know who it is but we bout to check it out.

We're not going to be scared in my own house." He straightened his back, put on his game face and said, "Follow me."

We rushed through the house finding our weapons of choice. Jay had the Brute spray deodorant with a lighter; it would be his flamethrower. Terrell had his bat and he wasn't in the mood to play any more. Derrell found our broom and I found the butcher's knife.

We heard more cracking leaves and fast footsteps. They slowed as they began to climb the stairs to the back door again. However, this time we were ready and before the intruder could touch the door again, Jay yelled, "Get'em!" As he threw open the back door and set that Brute spray on fire almost barbecuing our next-door neighbor, Mr Roosevelt.

"Aww!" screamed Mr Roosevelt as the flames came dangerously close to singeing off is eyebrows. He leaped of the porch screaming, "You dang kids, you're crazy! I was just checking on you like yo' ma said too." Then he stormed away. We quietly went back inside, closed and locked the door.
I believe we were all more afraid than we wanted to say. A few minutes passed and then this roar of laughter filled the bedroom as tears fell out our eyes, recanting what had just occurred and how crazy Mr Roosevelt was looking.

We never finished our game and we never put

up our weapons but we feel asleep laughing about
our little adventure. We hope you enjoyed this story; it
is one of many.

LIFE
By: MGM (Melagriggs2005)

THE MORNING DEW REPRESENTS TIME AS IT IS FRESH AND NEW.

THE NOON SUN SHINES ON THE STRENGTH OF THE YOUNG.

THE EVENING SKY, MIXES HUES, LIKE THE LOVERS IN NUDE.

THE RISING MOON, NOW WISDOM'S PERFUME.

AS THE MIDNIGHT SKY PLAYS YOUR FINAL TUNE.

We all die.
The goal isn't to live forever,
the goal is to
create something that will.
Chuck Palahniuk

Bravo
By: Jizammie J. Griggs

Death is life's last laugh, leaving us without a retort or encore.
No two performances are the same, not in time, style or flair.
Life is riddling and uncertain yet its reality is brutal and harsh.
Leaving those behind to mourn in its aftermath, and this
Could easily be a blessing for the ones that passed,
For they no longer have to suffer, through the pains in which
Life pranksters, it catches its victims off guard, and most of
The time unprepared to deal with existence's cruel humor,
Which leaves you not to perform in such high splendor,
But hobbled and humbled with agony, from the practical
Jokes of life with death being its final act. It is not rewarded
By applause or appraisal, but by tears and sorrow, for every
Death affects many lives, and these lives join in with the crowd

Of anti-celebration, which is equivalent to a standing ovation,
Leaving one to utter Bravo, Bravo: What a performance.

Dedicated to my friend, Mike Seavy
By: Officer Jay Griggs

True love is a meeting of two souls, fully accepting the dark and the light within each other, bound by the courage to grow through struggle into bliss.
Unknown

True Love
By: Meccia G McCants 9th October 2015

Developing slowly,

This love within forming.

The swell of new life.

Each change a delight.

Soon time for releasing.

My desire increasing.

Flesh is being strained,

Pressure insane,

Tears fall like rain,

Loving thoughts in my brain.

Excitement and fear,

Pleasure and pain.

All these emotions,

Real life versus notions

Chaos turns to joy.

True love has been born.

The Fate of Pretty
By: Jizammie J. Griggs

Pretty is not a commodity, in fact pretty, pretty much is saturated. Everyone is trying to be pretty, get pretty or become prettier and continue to fail! Pretty has an expiration date! I saw a girl today that wasn't as pretty as she was yesterday! OK
And no I'm not one of the pretties, but I've had my fair share of the pretty ones. And I can tell you they are much more insecure than us 'Normal People!' But we won't discriminate against them, we will welcome them in! But a word of advice, to the pretty people! Bring more to the table than just a pretty face!
Now some of you will read this and assume that you're one of the pretties, and you just might be! But time will pass and pictures will fade and your grade will fall, you'll see, and then you will take your rightful place, as a 'Normal Person!' Just like me!

My Heart
By: Meccia G. McCants 27th May 2015

Not once did I stop to think.

Not once did I fear.

You needed my love and so,

Here it is.

Don't be like the others,

Who came, took, and strayed.

But stay with great tenderness,

And when needed, offer aid.

I'm asking too much,

I know it's not fair.

So if you must wonder,

Please leave my heart here,

That I may be freed from dying this year.

From the Outside Looking in
By: Meccia G. McCants 19th November 2015

We see one another and smile

With the glow of a child in our eyes.

The innocence of love fills our hearts,

But we fear arrows of the past that with

Precision brings hurts that last.

From the outside we seem the pair to win,

To forever soar on the wind,

But inside you see wounded, bruised and battered,

I see frightened, marred and discontent.

From outside we are a powerhouse,

Fortified and sagacious

But in here we are haunted with ghost

Of hours passing, of years no longer laughing,

Of love no longer made, this friendship begins to fade.

But from the outside looking in, we're lovers and best friends.

Thank you Jesus
By: Jizammie J. Griggs

Easter Poem

Easter, new life, sacrifice, forgiveness, and renewal!
Jesus gladly gave his life,
For us, yes he sacrificed,
Paid our debt by shedding his blood,
Let us never doubt his love,
Jesus Christ is a gift from high above,
Now don't be sad this was not the end,
For in just three days he rose my friend,
Our sinful debt has now been paid,
Let gratitude guide the rest of your days!
For he is God's only begotten son,
And without his life, we would have none.
Now bow your head as true believers
And repeat after me, Thank you Jesus.

Poem written for my daughter,
Allison Leona-Diamond Griggs
Jizammie J. Griggs

Simply Me (My Heart's Response to God)
By: Meccia G. McCants 25th January 2016

The day I came to know the truth of how wonderful
you are;
I found for the first time, I was simply being me.
No facades, no hidden cares; I was smiling.
Did I dare find the time to rest; to simply be me?

Who knew how freeing the hours of being,
When deception not masking
your honest reactions
To the quirks of my person
and the malformations of my mind.
You received me fully
and now I know, I can be simply me.

Majestic explorations could not reveal
The marvel I failed to know;
The secret concealed,
In being loved so dearly, for simply being,
Me.

Claim
By: Meccia G. McCants 21st January 2016

It is not in you I see the vision, the light, the truth;
For that all reside in a Faith, I don't have in you.
Not negating that you are my love, my friend, my dear;
But you tend to only hold me so near.

At times you leave me rejected; abandoned in fear,
Drowning in the swell of emotions and tears.
The waterfall of pain, neglect; it's real,
But I'm staking my claim to us.
I'm gaining my strength for this ordained love.

The darkness may seep in, bringing the vices of sin;
As the wolf with a grin, threatening to alter our end.
But I will fulfill my lover's vow,
With my faith, I'll hold us down.
For we are anchored in my Master's care,
Till death do us part; I claim you my dear.

Hype
By: Jizammie J. Griggs

As we graduate, to the level of friends, I pray for this, to never end, as countless days, and nights pass by, magnetic splendor, enlightens my mind, of thoughts of you, your zone shines through, to capture heaven, I picture you, with lacy textures, I scream your name, experiencing pleasures, along with pain, as my frantic heartbeat, ignites my fears, of calling you sweetheart, darling and dear. With gentle patience, I wait for you, to accept my love, which exhibits true, I am all the man, that I can be. But without you, I am incomplete, I ponder on, what could have been, but understand, it's not the end, with absolute, faith in thee, I am hype about, what's soon to be. You and me, sharing endless times, I admit true love, is hard to find, but within you, I've claimed my goal, a person to match, my heart and soul, and as I stare, into your eyes, a light brown feature, is my surprise, and within this, I've uncovered the truth, and it leaves me hype, about me and you.

www.ingramcontent.com/pod-product-compliance
Lightning Source LLC
LaVergne TN
LVHW041553060526
838200LV00037B/1262